churchill

Meet the Family

My Aunt and Uncle

by Mary Auld

Gareth Stevens Publishing
A WORLD ALMANAC EDUCATION GROUP COMPANY

This is Nell and her brother Simon with their Aunt Sue and Uncle Clive. Sue is Nell and Simon's dad's sister, and Clive is her husband.

Paul and Dina's mom has a younger brother, Anthony. Anthony is Paul and Dina's uncle. Paul is Anthony's nephew, and Dina is Anthony's niece.

Will has four aunts and seven uncles. Here they all are with Will's mom.

Sally's aunt Christine is not related to her at all. She is Sally's mom's best friend.

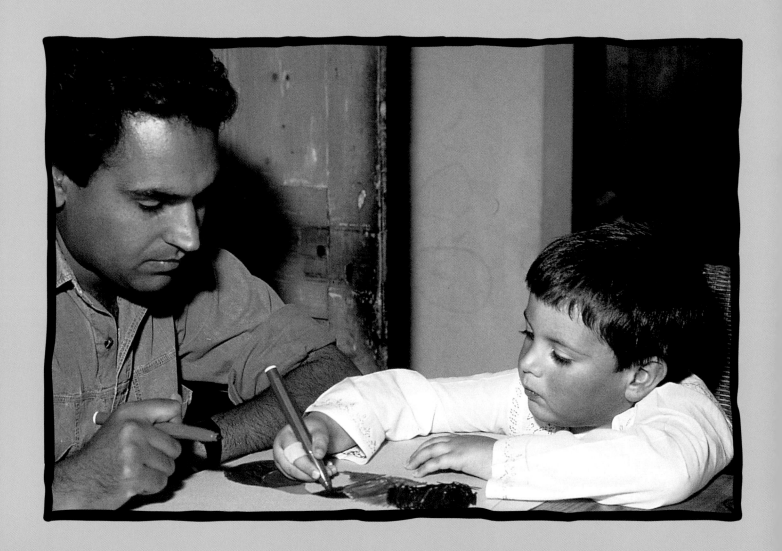

When Oliver's parents go out, his uncle often babysits him.

Rob's uncle runs
his own business.

Shanti's aunt is a student.

Duncan's aunt takes her
nephew out for the day.

Clarice's uncle and aunt taught her to ride a bike.

Alice and Penny
take a vacation
with their uncle
and aunt.

Rob likes talking
to his aunt about
many things.

Lucy likes playing with her cousins, who are the children of her aunts and uncles.

Tom and his dad are with Tom's great-uncle Jack and great-aunt Naomi. They are Tom's dad's uncle and aunt.

Do you have an aunt or uncle? What are they like?

Family Words

Here are some words people use when talking about their aunts, uncles, or family.

uncle, aunt, nephew, niece.

Names for parents:
father, daddy, dad, papa,
mother, mommy, mom, mama.

Names of other relatives:
sister, brother, daughter, son,
grandchild, grandparent,
grandma, grandmother,
grandpa, grandfather.

A great-relative is someone who is separated from us by an extra generation. Look at the family tree on page 24. Each level on it is a generation.

A Family Tree

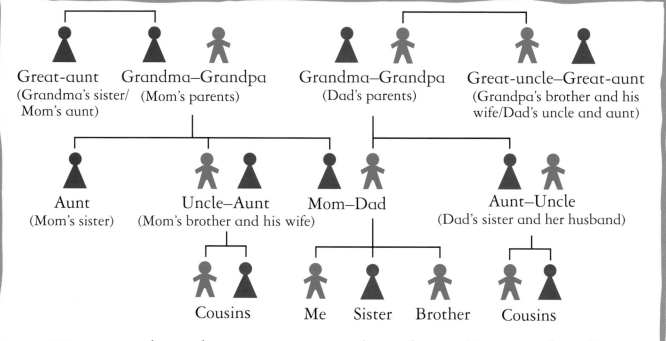

Great-aunt (Grandma's sister/ Mom's aunt) — Grandma–Grandpa (Mom's parents) — Grandma–Grandpa (Dad's parents) — Great-uncle–Great-aunt (Grandpa's brother and his wife/Dad's uncle and aunt)

Aunt (Mom's sister) — Uncle–Aunt (Mom's brother and his wife) — Mom–Dad — Aunt–Uncle (Dad's sister and her husband)

Cousins — Me — Sister — Brother — Cousins

You can show how you are related to all your family on a plan like this one. It is called a family tree. Every family tree is different. Try drawing your own.

Please visit our web site at: www.garethstevens.com
For a free color catalog describing Gareth Stevens Publishing's list of high-quality books and multimedia programs, call 1-800-542-2595 (USA) or 1-800-387-3178 (Canada). Gareth Stevens Publishing's fax: (414) 332-3567.

Library of Congress Cataloging-in-Publication Data available upon request from publisher. Fax (414) 336-0157 for the attention of the Publishing Records Department.

ISBN 0-8368-3923-4

This North American edition first published in 2004 by **Gareth Stevens Publishing**, A World Almanac Education Group Company, 330 West Olive Street, Suite 100, Milwaukee, WI 53212 USA

This U.S. edition copyright © 2004 by Gareth Stevens, Inc. First published in 2003 by Franklin Watts, 96 Leonard Street, London EC2A 4XD. Original copyright © 2003 by Franklin Watts.

Series editor: Rachel Cooke
Art director: Jonathan Hair
Design: Andrew Crowson
Gareth Stevens editor: Betsy Rasmussen
Gareth Stevens art direction: Tammy Gruenewald

Picture Credits: Bruce Berman/Corbis: front cover center. www.johnbirdsall.co.uk: front cover center below, 1, 6, 9, 15, 18, 19. Jackie Chapman/Photofusion: 13. Carlos Goldin/ Corbis: front cover center above. Sally Greenhill/Sally & Richard Greenhill PL: 16-17. Judy Harrison/Format: 10. David Montford/Photofusion: 2. Jose Luis Pelaez/Corbis: front cover top. Ulrike Preuss/Format: 14. David Raymer/Corbis: 12. George Shelley/Corbis: front cover bottom, 5. Ariel Skelley/Corbis: front cover main, 22. Jeff Zaruba Studio/Corbis: 20-21. While every attempt has been made to clear copyright, should there be any inadvertent omission please notify the publisher regarding rectification.

Printed in Hong Kong/China

1 2 3 4 5 6 7 8 9 08 07 06 05 04